Getting To Know...

Nature's Children

LYNX

Merebeth Switzer

SCHOLASTIC INC.

New York Toronto London Auckland Sydney
Mexico City New Delhi Hong Kong Buenos Aires

Facts in Brief

Classification of the Lynx

    Class: *Mammalia* (mammals)

    Order: *Carnivora* (meat-eaters)

    Family: *Felidae* (cat family)

    Genus: *Lynx*

    Species: *Lynx lynx*

World distribution. North American subspecies are exclusive to North America; other subspecies are found in Europe, Asia, and North Africa.

Habitat. Thickly forested areas.

Distinctive physical characteristics. Short body with long legs and large feet; short thick black-tipped tail; long tufts of fur on ears; black markings on face.

Habits. Solitary; active at night; usually occupies a "home range" year-round if there is an available food supply.

Diet. Birds and small mammals.

Published by Scholastic Inc.
90 Old Sherman Turnpike, Danbury, Connecticut 06816.

SCHOLASTIC and associated logos are trademarks of Scholastic Inc.

ISBN 0-7172-6701-6

Printed in the U.S.A.

Edited by: Elizabeth Grace Zuraw
Photo Rights: Ivy Images

Photo Editor: Nancy Norton
Cover Design: Niemand Design

Have you ever wondered . . .

If you took a walk through the northern woods, you could be near a lynx without even knowing it. The lynx might be peering out from under the low branches of an alder bush or it might be looking down at you from its perch high up in a spruce tree. But however unaware you might be of the lynx, you can be sure that this alert cat would know *you* were there.

Lynx are the "ghost cats" of the northern woods. They're rarely seen, except at night, and as soon as they are spotted, they disappear in a fast-moving blur.

Although there's something mysterious about the lynx, there's also something very familiar about it. Perhaps that's because it's a distant relative of our pet cats. Let's take a closer look at the lynx and discover more about this shy and secretive, but beautiful, wildcat.

One look at a lynx, and there's no mistaking it: This animal is a member of the cat family.

Playtime

Young lynx are a lot like people's pet kittens. In fact, they're sometimes called kittens. And like all young cats, they love to play. They'll leap out of the shadows at each other, tussle head over heels in the morning sunshine, and then they might suddenly give that up and turn to swat a horsefly buzzing by. They'll scratch a nearby stump and then pounce, tumble, jump, run…and they're back at the den where their mother is snoozing. After all that playing, the kittens are tired, too. It's time to nestle into their mother's soft silky fur for a quick catnap.

Lynx kittens are fluffy balls of curiosity and playfulness.

The "Who's Who" of Wildcats

There are three wildcats in North America: the cougar, the bobcat, and the lynx. The largest of the three is the cougar, also called the mountain lion or puma, and it's the easiest to recognize. It has a distinct sandy-brown coat, a black muzzle, and a long tail.

The other two North American wildcats are the lynx and the bobcat—the cougar's smaller relatives. You can tell the difference between a lynx and bobcat by looking at their tails. Both have short stumpy tails, but they have different markings. The lynx has a single, solid black tip on its tail. The bobcat's tail has a black tip, too, but it has an additional four or five dark rings around it, and it's somewhat longer.

You can also tell the lynx from the bobcat by its size, coat, and ears. Generally, the lynx is larger, has longer legs, and has fewer spots on its coat than the bobcat. It also has longer, far more distinctive tufts, or pointed clumps, of fur on its ears.

Despite these differences, it still can be tricky to tell these cats apart. For a quick identification of "who's who," it's probably best to focus on the ears and tail.

Lynx tail

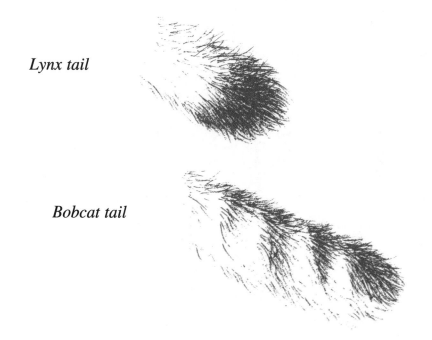

Bobcat tail

Lynx Around the World

North American lynx have close cousins in Europe and Asia. Most lynx live in northern forest country. Some live still farther north, in the *tundra,* the treeless plains found in arctic regions. But even these northerly lynx stay in shrub-covered areas where they can hide from enemies and also avoid, until the last possible moment, being seen by *prey,* the animals they hunt for food.

Opposite page: *The secretive lynx, preferring to remain hidden, seeks the cover of dense brush, trees, or even just an old stump.*

Where lynx live in North America

Lean and Lanky

The lynx has long legs and huge paws. These features make the animal seem much larger than it really is. Actually, the lynx weighs only 18 to 25 pounds (8 to 11 kilograms), which is about the same weight as a one-year-old baby. Just think—if the lynx were willing, you could probably pick it up easily in your arms!

As with most animals, male lynx are larger than the females. And in northern areas, lynx may grow slightly bigger than their cousins who live more to the south.

Along with a short black-tipped tail and tufted ears, huge snowshoe feet are the marks of a lynx.

Because of its husky build, the lynx is a little awkward when it runs, but it's very light on its feet when it walks.

Snowshoes and Long-jump Legs

The lynx's long legs, over-sized paws, and furry toes all play important roles in the lynx's survival. They help the animal move quickly and easily, even in deep snow.

Thanks to its extra long legs, the lynx covers a great distance with each stride. Although it usually gallops along rather clumsily, it can move very quickly if it has to. Having powerful legs also means the lynx can leap gracefully over small thickets and fallen trees in the forest. In winter, the lynx's massive feet act like snowshoes. How? The furry toes spread far apart to distribute the lynx's weight out over the snow so that the animal doesn't sink in. Furry toes also help keep its feet warm. At temperatures of 30 degrees below zero Fahrenheit (35 degrees below zero Celsius), warm feet are pretty important!

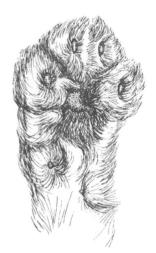

Front paw

Hind paw

15

Two Coats Are Better Than One

Opposite page:
The guard hairs in a lynx's coat can be 4 inches (10 centimeters) in length. That's longer than a new crayon!

Because the lynx is active all year long, it needs two coats: a cool one for summer, and a warm one for winter.

The lynx's summer coat is quite short, but even so, on hot days the lynx heads for a shady spot. There it lies down and sometimes even pants like a dog to cool off. This summer fur is light brown with faint spots. The brownish color and mottled pattern help the lynx blend into the shadows of the summer forest. In the fall, the lynx slowly sheds its summer fur. At the same time, a buffy gray winter coat with even fainter spots is growing in. The lynx's winter coat has two layers. The layer closest to the skin is a dense *underfur* that works like a woolen blanket to keep in body warmth.

The underfur is covered by an outer layer of long, black-tipped *guard hairs* that protect the lynx from icy winds and shed water, too.

A Natural Hunter

Cats are some of the world's best equipped hunters, and the lynx is no exception. Its keen senses and strong, agile body, as well as its powerful jaws and sharp teeth, make it a very successful hunter indeed.

Just like a pet cat, the lynx, on soft padded feet, sneaks up silently on its prey. The lynx seems to know just where to step to make the least noise. It knows that even the tiniest snapping of a twig could cost it its dinner. If you've ever watched a house cat step gracefully around a row of houseplants or through a display of china ornaments, you've seen how well a cat can do this.

When it gets close to its prey, the lynx waits. Then, quick as a flash, it bounds: one, two, three—success! The lynx won't be hungry tonight.

Stalking in complete silence before pouncing on prey is the lynx's main way of hunting.

The Hare Connection

The lynx hunts mice, voles, squirrels, and grouse, and even feeds on dead deer and caribou calves. But in winter, it depends mainly on Snowshoe Hares, which may make up three quarters or more of the lynx's diet.

Scientists have discovered that when there are only a few hares, there are only a few lynx. Then the numbers of both animals slowly begin to increase as each has a more plentiful food supply. When the hares have lots of plants to munch on, the lynx have lots of hares to hunt. But quite regularly after about ten years, there are too many Snowshoe Hares for the amount of food available to them. So the number of hares begins to drop, and as it does, so, too, does the number of lynx. Then this ten-year cycle begins again....

In winter, Lynx spend a good deal of their time watching for the chance to catch a Snowshoe Hare for dinner.

Look Out Below!

The lynx is an excellent climber, and it often selects a tall tree for a lookout. From up in the tree it can spot prey without being seen.

It also climbs trees to escape if it's being chased by a wolf. The lynx's climbing ability is less help, however, if it's being trailed by another of its enemies, the cougar. A cougar can climb trees just as easily as a lynx. Like most cats, the lynx doesn't like getting wet. But it'll do anything to escape a cougar— even jump into the water and swim!

Overleaf:
A lynx may appear to be resting, but it's ever alert to its surroundings.

Lynx like to climb trees and stretch out on a limb. They also use the high vantage point to search out prey.

Night Vision

Because the lynx usually hunts at night, it has extra-sensitive vision to help it find food. Like most cats, it can see well, even in the dark. Its sense of smell, however, is not as good as its eyesight.

The next time you meet a cat, take a look at its special eyes. You'll notice that the *pupil,* the black part in the center, changes size rapidly. In bright sunlight, it's a tiny slit, but in the dark, the pupil opens into a large dark circle. This opening allows more light to come into the eye so that the cat can see better.

The lynx sees only in black and white and shades of gray. But even though it can't see colors, it probably sees as well on a moonlit night as you do in broad daylight.

Lynx eye
in sunlight

Not accustomed to bright daylight,
a lynx squints against the sun.

Whisker Warnings

The lynx doesn't rely totally on its eyes for hunting. It uses its shoulder-width face whiskers, too. When the lynx is winding its way through thick underbrush or dark caves and the tips of its whiskers brush against something, the lynx stops to size up the situation. Like other cats, it knows that if its whiskers can't fit through an opening, the rest of its body won't be able to squeeze through, either.

A lynx's whiskers are sensitive feelers that give the animal important information about its surroundings.

Trespassers, Keep Out!

Male lynx claim hunting *territories,* or areas, which they defend against other males. How do lynx know whose territory belongs to whom? Each lynx marks his territory with special signs. To do this the male reaches high up on a tree trunk and scratches, sharpening his claws and at the same time leaving behind gouges in the wood. He then raises his hind leg and urinates against the tree, just as a dog does at a fire hydrant. A tree marked in this way is known as a *scent post* or *scrape,* and it lets other lynx know, "This territory is taken. Stay out!"

These scent posts are marked regularly as the lynx makes a nightly tour over a wide network of trails. Down the river bank he pads, up a rocky slope, along a cliff ridge, and across a deserted logging road. The lynx may travel as many as 12 miles (19 kilometers) each night, marking his territory as he goes.

Tree clawed by a lynx

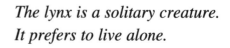

The lynx is a solitary creature. It prefers to live alone.

The lynx has little choice but to keep its area marked. If the scent on a scent post were to fade, another lynx might move in and take over the territory.

The female lynx doesn't seem to be as concerned about claiming a special territory. Instead she's allowed to move in and out of the males' territories. Who knows—she might even prove to be a mate when *mating season* arrives! Mating season is the time of year during which animals come together to produce young. But even though the male doesn't consider a female to be a threat to his territory, it's not because she's weak. Quite to the contrary, a female lynx can and will fiercely fight a male challenger, especially when she has young to defend.

Male and female lynx live peacefully in the same territory. But a male is careful to protect his territory from other males.

Winning a Mate

Opposite page: *While the males fight it out, the female is not far away. She'll answer the victor's mating call with her own special yowls and purrs.*

During mating season—between January and March—a male lynx's howls fill the night air. These distinct howls attract females and challenge any other male who ventures into his territory. What a noisy ruckus! If you've ever heard a pair of tomcats yowling in your backyard, you can imagine the sound that echoes through the forest when two large male lynx are howling.

Because the drive to father the next generation is strong, two males often fight to see who will win a female. These catfights can be fierce. The two males, spitting and screaming at each other, soon become a ball of flashing claws and flying fur. Who will win? In the end, the weaker male leaves the fight before he suffers any life-threatening injuries. He skulks off into the bush, leaving the stronger and healthier cat to father the young. This process helps to insure that the babies, too, will be strong and healthy.

A Not-so-dutiful Dad

Sometimes the male and the female lynx remain together for a few weeks to hunt and play. However, many males will leave their mate and look for yet another female to bear their young.

Even if the male lynx does stay with the female, she will drive him away long before the kittens are born. Male lynx are dangerous to kittens and have even been known to kill their own. Sometimes the male doesn't want to leave, but the female's hisses, bites, and threats soon get her message across.

A lynx pair may stay together after mating, but the mother raises her young alone. Lynx babies are born about two months after the parents mate.

Opposite page:
Lynx kittens are not helpless for long. Within two months they are sporting new coats and exploring the world.

Mother Knows Best

Like many mothers, a lynx mother is very protective of her young. She keeps her kittens' birth and the location of her *den,* or home, a secret from the male—and from everyone else, too. But we do know some things about the lynx from studying the behavior of its close cousins.

About two months after mating, the mother finds a secluded den. Because she cares for the kittens by herself, she needs a safe home with good hunting grounds nearby. After a search, she selects a site that might be under the low branches of a spruce tree, inside a rotten log, or in a dark dry cave.

When the mother lynx gives birth, there are anywhere from one to five kittens in her *litter,* the name of the young animals that are born together. At birth, the tiny kittens are helpless gray balls of fluffy fur. They cannot see or hear, but within the next two weeks their eyes open and their hearing develops.

Growing Up Fast

Although baby lynx are only slightly larger than pet kittens, their large lynx paws are already quite big. For the first few weeks, the babies remain in the den and *nurse,* or drink the rich milk in their mother's body. Although the mother leaves them regularly to hunt for dinner, she's always nearby. She never knows when another lynx or a cougar or wolf might find her babies, and she needs to be on hand to protect them.

Sometimes the mother lynx returns from her hunting trip with a treat for her kittens— a juicy bone or a piece of meat. Gnawing on bones strengthens the kittens' jaws. And an occasional piece of meat gives them a taste of what they'll soon be hunting for.

By the age of two months, lynx kittens have lost the gray fluff they were born with. They now have rich red or buff-colored coats, dappled with soft brown spots. The active and curious kittens are into everything, and are constantly at play in a steady stream of hide and seek, chase and pounce, tumble and tussle.

Practice Makes Perfect

Playing prepares the kittens for one of the most important parts of their lives: hunting for food. At two months the young lynx not only are sharing parts of their mother's meal, but they are ready to join her on her nightly hunts. The sooner they learn how to catch their food, the better for all.

The female hides her young nearby while she stalks her prey, and the kittens learn how to hunt by watching their mother. Soon they're trying to catch their own dinner. They start with something small, perhaps a mouse or a vole. And just as you probably do when you're learning something new, they make a lot of mistakes at first. But day by day their hunting skills improve.

A lynx kitten learns all the details of successful hunting from its watchful mother.

Clean as a Whistle

The kittens grow rapidly, and by autumn they are almost as big as their mother. For the first time, they shed their summer fur, and a new thick winter coat grows in. Their long adult fur makes the kittens look very much like their elegant parents.

A beautiful coat needs special care. For their first five months, the kittens' mother gives them thorough daily baths with her rough tongue to keep the youngsters clean. Now the young lynx must wash and *groom,* or clean, their own fur. Cleaning their coats on a regular basis keeps the fur healthy, so that it'll keep the young lynx warm during the long winter.

A young lynx has many survival lessons to learn. But taking time to rest is important, too.

Family Farewells

The temperature drops down lower and lower each autumn night. The days get shorter and shorter, and soon the first snows begin to fall in the northern woods. But the young lynx will be cozy—they'll stay with their mother through much of the winter.

In late winter or early spring, the lynx family splits up. The mother doesn't want her young around when she mates again. Besides, the young are now able to look after themselves. The family will never be together again, but by next spring, the young lynx will be ready to start their own families.

Until then, each of these beautiful and mysterious cats will prowl through the northern forests. They might suddenly leap out of nowhere—and in an instant, they may be gone again, vanishing like shadows into the depths of the night.

Words To Know

Den   An animal home.

Groom   To clean and brush.

Guard hairs   Long coarse hairs that make up the outer layer of a lynx's coat.

Litter   The young animals that are born together.

Mate   To come together to produce young. Either member of an animal pair is also the other's mate.

Mating Season   The time of year during which animals mate.

Nurse   To drink the milk from a mother's body.

Prey   An animal hunted by another animal for food.

Pupil   The opening in the center of the eye which controls the amount of light taken in.

Scent post or **scrape**   Special signs that mark the boundaries of an animal's territory.

Territory   The area that an animal or group of animals lives in and often defends from other animals of the same kind.

Tundra   Treeless plains in arctic regions.

Underfur   Thick short hair that traps body-warmed air next to a lynx's skin.

Index

Getting To Know...

Nature's Children

SEA LIONS

Mark Shawver

SCHOLASTIC INC.

New York   Toronto   London   Auckland   Sydney
Mexico City   New Delhi   Hong Kong   Buenos Aires

Facts in Brief

Classification of North American sea lions

      Class: *Mammalia* (mammals)

      Order: *Pinnipedia* (pinnipeds)

      Family: *Otariidae* (eared seals)

      Genus: *Eumetopias* (Northern Sea Lion)

                Zalophus (California Sea Lion)

      Species: *Eumetopias jubata* (Northern Sea Lion)

                Zalophus californianus (California Sea Lion)

World distribution. Both species are found in the coastal waters on both sides of the Pacific Ocean in the Northern Hemisphere.

Habitat. Coastal waters; shore.

Distinctive physical characteristics. Strong front flippers for swimming; rear flippers that can be turned forward for walking on land.

Habits. Lives in herds; playful in water; migrates seasonally.

Diet. Squid, octopus, fish, shell fish.

Published by Scholastic Inc.
90 Old Sherman Turnpike, Danbury, Connecticut 06816.

SCHOLASTIC and associated logos are trademarks of Scholastic Inc.

ISBN 0-7172-6701-6

Printed in the U.S.A.

Edited by: Elizabeth Grace Zuraw

Photo Rights: Ivy Images

Photo Editor: Nancy Norton

Cover Design: Niemand Design

Have you ever wondered . . .

If you were to come upon a herd of Sea Lions, you'd know it even before you saw them. They're noisy! As they lie about or frolic in the sun or clamber over each other on their way down to the ocean, they're never quiet and they're seldom still. A *colony* of Sea Lions is a mighty busy place. Colony is the name for a group of the same kind of animals living together.

Unfortunately, the only Sea Lions most people see are trained ones in aquarium shows—the ones that balance balls on their noses, blow horns, and clap their flippers on command. So let's take a look and see how these fascinating creatures—so clumsy on land, yet so graceful in the water—live in the wild.

When ashore, Sea Lions often gather in crowded colonies.

Puppy Love

Imagine yourself as a baby Sea Lion on a crowded beach where hundreds of Sea Lions have gathered. The world is still very new and you have much to learn. Suddenly, you hear the thunderous growling of two enormous Sea Lions fighting each other. You look up and see that one of them has been given a huge shove and is rolling your way. You're certain to be crushed! But at the last second, you're grabbed by the neck and yanked away to safety. Although you were unaware of it, your mother has been watching over you carefully and has come to your rescue.

Scenes like this happen quite often. For the first five or six months of a Sea Lion's life, its mother is nearby, ready to protect it. Mother and baby spend much of their time lying on the beach, snuggling close together. The little one, called a *pup,* especially enjoys stretching out on its mother's back for an afternoon nap.

A Sea Lion pup stays close to its mother.

Fin-footed

Sea Lions belong to a group of animals called *pinnipeds,* a word that means "fin-footed." They were given this name because their feet are effective swimming fins.

Pinnipeds can be divided into three groups. Sea Lions and their close cousins, the Fur Seals, are called eared seals. All other seals are called earless seals. And both kinds of seals are related to the third kind of pinniped, the walrus.

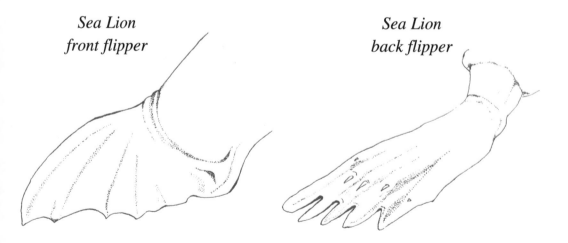

Sea Lion front flipper

Sea Lion back flipper

The Sea Lion's long, flat flippers make for easy, swift, and often acrobatic swimming.

Seal or Sea Lion?

What's the difference between a Sea Lion and most seals? The easiest way to tell them apart is to compare their ears and the way they walk. If the animal has no visible ear flaps and crawls on the land on its stomach like a big caterpillar, it's a seal. If it has small ears on the sides of its head and walks on its four flippers, it's a Sea Lion or a Fur Seal.

There are two kinds of Sea Lions along the coast of North America—the Northern Sea Lion and the more common California Sea Lion. The Northern Sea Lion is also known as the Steller Sea Lion. It was named after Georg Steller, a German scientist who first discovered the animal more than 200 years ago.

A Sea Lion has tiny ear flaps on both sides of its head.

Where They Live

In North America, Sea Lions can be found on the West Coast all the way from the cold waters of Alaska's Bering Sea to the warm tropical waters off California and Mexico. Northern Sea Lions prefer rocky shores, while California Sea Lions like sand or boulder beaches backed by cliffs.

During the fall and winter, the males travel great distances in search of better fishing areas. The females usually stay fairly close to the *breeding grounds,* or places where they give birth to pups and teach them how to take care of themselves.

*Where Sea
Lions live in
North America*

■ Northern Sea Lion

■ California Sea Lion

12

Super Swimmers

A Sea Lion is certainly at its best in the water. Every movement is graceful as it spins and twirls in an underwater ballet. Several thrusts of its flippers can send the Sea Lion gliding through the water at speeds of about 15 to 20 miles (24 to 32 kilometers) per hour.

The Sea Lion's large paddle-like front flippers are about as long as a man's arm. These flippers flap up and down much like the wings of a bird.

Sea Lions can't breathe underwater so they have to swim to the water's surface when they need air.

On the Move

A Sea Lion uses its shorter hind flippers to steer in the water. On land the hind flippers bend forward and are used for walking.

Sea Lions are great divers and enjoy leaping from rocks or boulders at the water's edge. But they must be very careful so they are not thrown against the rocks by crashing waves.

The Sea Lion's torpedo-shaped body helps make it one of nature's most skilled swimmers. Its streamlined body glides almost effortlessly through the water.

A Sea Lion uses all four flippers for getting around on land.

A Fishy Feast

Sea Lions get all of their food from the ocean. They enjoy meals of herring and other kinds of fish.

Sea Lions feed mostly at night—and they have to move quickly to catch their slippery meals. They capture their *prey,* or the animals they hunt for food, and hold it tightly in their powerful jaws. Sea Lions rarely chew their food. Instead they swallow it whole. If a fish is too big to be swallowed in one gulp, the Sea Lion shakes it vigorously to break it into bite-sized pieces.

Usually Sea Lions hunt by themselves or with a few companions. But when a *school,* or group, of herring swims by, many Sea Lions join in the hunt. Even Sea Lions enjoying an afternoon nap wake up to take part in the fishy feast.

Sometimes a Sea Lion chases a fish just for the fun of it. It'll catch the fish, let it go, chase it around some more, and then let it go again. Sea Lions seem to enjoy this game!

Opposite page: *A Sea Lion's menu includes fish such as cod, flounder, and greenling. It also eats squid and octopus.*

Overleaf: *Sea Lions "haul out" onto rocky shores to rest.*

19

Heavy Weights

Did you know that some Sea Lions may grow to be the size of a small car? In fact, the Northern Sea Lion may weigh up to 2,000 pounds (900 kilograms) and reach a length of about 9 feet (3 meters). The average California Sea Lion, however, is much smaller. It weighs about 550 pounds (250 kilograms) and measures about 8 feet (2.5 meters) long. The females are only about one-third the weight of the males.

Male, or *bull,* Sea Lions are usually brown in color. The females, or *cows,* are a lighter shade of brown. But when their fur gets wet, both male and female Sea Lions look almost black.

Sea Lions may start life tiny, but some grow to be larger than an adult Polar Bear.

23

Cozy Warm

The Sea Lion has several ways of staying warm even in chilly waters. A thick layer of fat, called *blubber,* lies under the Sea Lion's skin. This layer of blubber keeps the animal's body heat in and the cold out.

The Sea Lion has another way of keeping warm. It grows a thick coat of fur. The hairs grow so close together that water never gets down to the animal's skin. Millions of tiny air bubbles trapped in the thick fur also help keep the cold out and the heat in.

In summer, Sea Lions can get too warm. To cool off, they may jump into the water. Other times they may pant like dogs or wave their flippers in the air like fans. The flippers don't have a layer of blubber, so heat from the Sea Lion's body can escape through them.

A fur coat is not a luxury for a Sea Lion. If the animal lives in icy northern waters, it's a necessity!

New Coats for Old

After a whole year of climbing on rocks, lying on rugged beaches, and fighting and playing, a Sea Lion's fur coat becomes quite ragged looking. The tattered fur no longer keeps the Sea Lion as warm as it once did. But no need to worry. Each spring when Sea Lions are on the beaches, their old fur falls out and new fur grows in. Because they're not in the water much at this time of year, missing some of their fur for a few weeks doesn't seem to bother them. This process of shedding old fur and growing a new coat is called *molting*. When a Sea Lion completes the process of molting, it sports a brand-new, beautiful, shiny coat of fur.

Sea Lions spend much time in the water,
but they also enjoy just loafing in the sun.

Underwater Eyes

If you were to dive deep into the ocean, you'd probably have trouble seeing. That's because deep down the oceans are dark and murky, and human eyes aren't suited to seeing in such conditions. A Sea Lion, however, has large eyes with pupils that open up wide to let in more light. This helps the animal see in the shadowy depths where human eyesight fails.

In addition, Sea Lions have a clear, protective layer that covers their open eyes when they're underwater. This layer is what gives a Sea Lion's eyes their soft, gentle look. Sea Lions also have eyelids much like our own that protect their eyes while on land. And on land, the Sea Lion's eyes are further protected by tears that help carry away sand or dirt. The tears flow freely down their cheeks, making it look as if Sea Lions are always crying.

"Seeing" in the Dark

If someone turned out the light in a room, how would you find your way around? You'd probably use your hands to feel your way. Well, the night-feeding Sea Lion often is in the dark when it hunts for fish underwater. But instead of using hands, it feels its way around with the help of its whiskers.

A Sea Lion's whiskers are controlled by tiny muscles, and are used much as you use your fingers to explore your surroundings. And the whiskers are equipped with sensitive nerves. Using them, a Sea Lion can tell a slippery octopus from a piece of wood. A trained Sea Lion can even use its whiskers to help balance a ball on the tip of its nose.

The Sea Lion's sensitive whiskers are an important part of its fishing gear.

Other Senses

When a Sea Lion is out of the water, it has a keen sense of smell. In fact, a mother Sea Lion can tell her pup from all others just by sniffing it. And a Sea Lion's nose is special underwater, too. The animal is able to close its nostrils so that it doesn't get a noseful of water when it dives and swims.

A Sea Lion's hearing also is excellent. This animal has short tube-like ears no bigger than your little toe, but these ears can pick up sounds underwater just as well as they do on land. Sea Lions cock their outer ear flaps much the way a dog does to focus sharply on incoming sounds.

A Sea Lion's sense of smell is useful only on land because its nostrils close up underwater.

Sea Dogs?

Sea Lions are very noisy animals, especially when they're gathered together on a beach. They make an "UHH, UHH" sound, and they growl and sometimes even bark. In fact, old-time sailors used to call them sea dogs.

A Sea Lion's bark can mean several things. A bull will bark loudly to warn other males to stay away from his *territory,* the area that an animal lives in and defends against other animals. The barking sound can also help a Sea Lion mother find a missing pup. She is able to tell her own infant's barking bleat from that of all the others, even though hundreds of pups may be barking at the same time.

Barking is also used as a warning signal. When danger is near, a bull barks rapidly as he runs toward the sea. He will soon be followed by other Sea Lions. Sea Lions bark under-water, too. This barking can be heard for long distances.

When a Sea Lion has something to communicate, it does so —loud and clear.

A Jungle Cry?

You may have wondered why these huge un-lion-like animals are called Sea Lions. All you'd have to do is hear a Northern Sea Lion roar and you'd instantly know why. If you closed your eyes while you listened, you'd think you were in the middle of a jungle, hearing a lion roar!

Baby Sea Lions make tiny sounds, but by the time the youngsters become adults, their voices become deep, loud, and bellowing.

Big Bullies

In the spring, with the arrival of warmer weather and longer days, Sea Lions begin to gather on beaches to give birth and to *mate,* or come together to produce young. The place where they gather is called a *rookery.*

Among California Sea Lions, the bulls arrive at the rookery first to claim an area of beach for themselves. This is their territory, and it's where their pups will be born. The females arrive later and settle in a bull's territory. In good territories, there may be 15 or more females. Among Northern Sea Lions, the females arrive first, followed by the bulls.

The group of females in one bull's territory is called a *harem.* The bull defends his territory by chasing off intruders. Very rarely do the bulls fight, but there is always a lot of barking and growling going on.

The males and females that are too young or too old to mate usually stay on the outskirts of the rookery. If they try to venture in, they're quickly chased away by one "big bully" after another.

Opposite page:
A common sight at a Sea Lion rookery is a bull ever alert to defend his territory.

Life on the Beach

Sea Lions mate in the summer while on the beaches and the female gives birth to a single pup the following year.

Opposite page:
*Young Sea Lions
cannot yet roar
or even bark.
Instead they bleat
or whimper like
young lambs.*

The newborn does not have a cozy nursery as some animals do. Instead, it's born right on the beach among hundreds of other Sea Lions.

The little one looks much like its mother, except that it is smaller and darker. The pup is about 33 to 39 inches (85 to 100 centimeters) long and weighs in at about 35 pounds (16 kilograms). Its eyes are wide open and it has a nice shiny coat of fur.

Within a few hours of its birth, the pup begins to *nurse,* or drink milk from its mother's body. Because this milk is very rich, the pup grows quickly. Although it will nurse for almost a year, the little Sea Lion starts eating fish at about six months.

The bull spends most of his time patrolling his territory and pays very little attention to the newborn pups.

On the Lookout

As they swim, hunt, and play in the ocean, Sea Lions don't have to be on the lookout for many *predators,* animals that hunt other animals for food. However, there are two enemies that the Sea Lion is always wary of. One is the shark and the other is the Killer Whale. In a fight with either of these two animals, even the largest of Sea Lions is almost defenseless. Its only chance is to swim fast or turn quickly to avoid the attacker.

If the Sea Lion can hide in a bed of under-water seaweed or make it to the beach, it may be safe. But it still has to be alert because Killer Whales sometimes slide a little way onto the shore to try to grab an unsuspecting Sea Lion.

Usually, the Sea Lion's enemies attack the sick or weak animals that are unable to swim fast enough to get away. Mother Sea Lions must be very watchful to protect their pups.

With its vigilant mother at its side, a Sea Lion pup is safe and carefree.

Swimming Lessons

How old were you when you took your first swimming lesson? Older than a Sea Lion, for sure. A Sea Lion starts swimming when it's only about ten days old! The pup follows its mother to a *tide pool,* a small pool close to the shore, where the water is shallow and calm. There mother and baby play together, staying near the pool's edge. If the pup gets tired, it often will climb up onto its mother's back for a rest.

The pup soon becomes expert in twisting and turning in the water. This skill is very important because the next lesson is how to catch a fish. The pup now has to learn when to breathe so that it won't take water into its lungs. When the mother finishes such a play-time lesson, she often carries the pup out of the water in her mouth.

After several weeks in the shallow tide pool, the pup is ready for deeper water, farther from shore. It quickly learns to dive below the crashing waves, closing its nose to keep the water out.

Opposite page:
Sea Lion pups never leave their mother's side for the first two weeks of their lives.

Challenges of the Deep

Young Sea Lions are very playful. They toss pebbles back and forth and chase each other around in the water, leaping and diving. They even play hide and seek in the underwater forest of seaweed and *kelp,* a type of underwater plant.

Since a pup's layer of blubber is very thin, the little Sea Lion can spend only short periods of time in the water. But as the pup gets older, the layer of blubber grows thicker, allowing the youngster to stay warm on longer swims.

By four months of age, most young Sea Lions are expert swimmers and can stay underwater for about seven minutes. By six months, the pup is ready to swim and hunt for fish on its own, although it stays close to its mother until the following spring. Then it takes its place on the outskirts of the rookery until it is ready to start a family of its own. In the wild, Sea Lions can live as many as 17 years and have many pups.

Words To Know

Blubber   A thick layer of fat just below a Sea Lion's skin.

Breeding grounds   Places where Sea Lions mate, give birth, and raise young.

Bull   A male Sea Lion.

Colony   A group of the same kind of animals living together.

Cow   A female Sea Lion.

Harem   A group of females in a bull's territory.

Kelp   A type of underwater plant, like seaweed.

Mate   To come together to produce young.

Molt   To shed one coat of fur or feathers and grow another.

Nurse   To drink milk from the mother's body.

Pinnipeds   A group of animals whose legs are specially shaped as flippers. Seals, Sea Lions, and walruses are pinnipeds.

Predator   An animal that hunts other animals for food.

Prey   An animal hunted by another animal for food.

Pup   A young Sea Lion.

Pupil   The part of the eye that gets larger or smaller depending on the amount of light.

Territory   An area that an animal lives in and defends from other animals of the same kind.

Tide pool   A small pool of water along a shore.

Rookery   An area on shore where Sea Lions go to mate, give birth, and raise their young.

School   A group of fish.

Index

PHOTO CREDITS
Cover: Herman Giethoorn, *Valan Photos.* **Interiors:** Barry Ranford, 4, 33. */Ivy Images:* Wayne Lynch, 6, 13. */Earth Views / Ivy Images:* Stephen Leatherwood, 9, 22-23; Gregory Silber, 18; Carlos Eyles, 29. */Canada In Stock / Ivy Images:* Frank S. Balthis, 10, 43. */Tom Stack & Associates:* Randy Morse, 14. */Bruno Kern, 17, 26. /Tim Fitzharris, 25, 34. /Valan Photos:* Hälle Flygare, 20-21. */J. D. Taylor, 30, 44. /Wayne Lynch, 36-37, 41. /Visuals Unlimited:* Bill Kamin, 38.